ideals
THANKSGIVING

Vol. 47, No. 7

Publisher, Patricia A. Pingry
Associate Editor, Nancy Skarmeas
Photography and Permissions Editor,
 Kathleen Gilbert
Art Director, Patrick McRae
Editorial Assistant, Fran Morley
Contributing Editor, Bonnie Aeschliman

ISBN 0-8249-1086-9

IDEALS—Vol. 47, No. 7 November MCMXC IDEALS
(ISSN 0019-137X) is published eight times a year: Febru-
ary, March, May, June, August, September, November,
December by IDEALS PUBLISHING CORPORATION,
P.O. Box 148000, Nashville, Tenn. 37214. Second-class
postage paid at Nashville, Tennessee, and additional
mailing offices. Copyright © MCMXC by IDEALS PUB-
LISHING CORPORATION. POSTMASTER: Send
address changes to Ideals, Post Office Box 148000,
Nashville, Tenn. 37214-8000. All rights reserved. Title
IDEALS registered U.S. Patent Office.

SINGLE ISSUE—$4.95
ONE-YEAR SUBSCRIPTION—eight consecutive issues as
published—$19.95
TWO-YEAR SUBSCRIPTION—sixteen consecutive issues
as published—$35.95
Outside U.S.A., add $6.00 per subscription year for postage
and handling.

FOREFATHERS' DAY from *LIVING THE YEARS* by
Edgar A. Guest. Copyright 1949 by The Reilly & Lee Co.
Used by permission of the Estate; THANKSGIVING FOR
NO from *THESE LOVELY DAYS* by Carol Bessent
Hayman, copyright 1971. Used by permission; PRAYER
IN AUTUMN from *NEW ENGLAND HERITAGE AND
OTHER POEMS* by Rose Koralewsky, copyright 1949.
Used by permission of Branden Publishing, Boston; THE
PACE THAT PASSES UNDERSTANDING and
THANKSGIVING from *ROADS WIDE WITH WONDER* by
Mary E. Linton. Copyright 1954 by Burton Publishing
Company. Used by permission of the author; I THANK
THEE from *EARTHBOUND NO LONGER* by Caroline
Eyring Miner, copyright 1961. Used by permission;
THANKSGIVING from *CHRISTMAS COULD-BE TALES
(And Other Verses)* by Margaret C. Rorke. Copyright
1984 by Northwood Press, Midland, MI. Used by
permission of the author; THIS IS AUTUMN from
MOMENTS OF SUNSHINE by Garnett Ann Schultz,
copyright © 1974. Used by permission. Our sincere
thanks to the following whose addresses we were unable
to locate: Angela Gall for GOING HOME; Mary McGowan
for CHRYSANTHEMUMS; the Estate of Elizabeth Lathrop
Powers for THANKFULNESS from *RYTHM ROAD*,
copyright 1951; BEING THANKFUL from HILLS OF
HOME by Myrtie Fisher Seaverns; TRANQUILITY from
BROWN LEAVES TURNING by Ora Pate Stewart,
copyright 1953; NOVEMBER from *SOME SMALL
DELIGHT* by Milly Walton, copyright 1949.

Four-color separations by Rayson Films, Inc., Waukesha,
Wisconsin

Printing by The Banta Company, Menasha, Wisconsin

The paper used in this publication meets the minimum
requirements of American National Standard for Information Sciences—Permanence of Paper for Printed
Library Materials, ANSI Z39.48-1984.

 Cover Photo
H. Armstrong Roberts

Harvesttime
FPG/Charles Marden Fitch

Thanksgiving Song

Wanda L. Jones

Autumn's chilly winds have come
To shake the thinning bough
And spread with gold the barren earth
That waits for springtime's plough.

The storage bins are bursting
With blessings from the field—
Fruit and grain and vegetables
From God's abundant yield.

The house is braced for winter's cold
With stores of winter wood.
The hearth's ablaze with hickory warmth:
The pungent air smells good.

Safe within, the loved ones sit:
Good cheer, good food, embraced.
Now thank we all our glorious God
For His bounty and His grace.

Slow Down, October

Peggy Mlcuch

The oak has turned golden,
   the sumac bright red—
The call of the wild geese
   resounds overhead.
The pumpkin patch basks in
   the glorious sun
And brilliant orange pumpkins
   proclaim work well-done.

The grapevines that wind o'er
   the crumbling stone wall
Hang clusters of fruit in
   earth's great harvest hall.
And the air's as crisp
   as the dry falling leaves,
And it makes me grateful, indeed,
   for my sweater's long sleeves.

While the wide, sun-bright sky
   with sapphire is hung
To catch wisps of clouds
   that Autumn has flung,
The hills that surround are
   intense in their hue
I gasp at their splendor—
   my faith I renew.

Oh, slow down October,
   we've need of your grace;
You cause us to pause in
   our maddening pace,
To rebuild old dreams that
   were once set aside
And take stock of the riches
   with which we abide.

East Topsham, Vermont
Dick Dietrich Photography

Photo Overleaf
Quaker Brook Farm
East Baldwin, Maine
Dick Dietrich Photography

Adam Jones, Photographer

This Is Autumn

Garnett Ann Schultz

This is a day for dreaming
For leaving cares behind,
For walking lovely country lanes
All bright and autumn-lined;

A day for life unhurried
In sunny meadows fair,
A field of golden beauty
With wonders everywhere.

Adam Jones, Photographer

This is a day for loving
The whole wide world aglow,
For finding magic splendor
In valleys far below,
The brilliant flame of sumac,
The cotton clouds on high,
An orchard soft and wistful
Beneath a peaceful sky.

This is a day for many things,
For hearts that laugh and love,
For drying leaves and blazing hills
And eyes that look above,
A country walk—a magic dream
An early setting sun,
For this is autumn hushed and still:
Autumn days have come.

Tranquility

Ora Pate Stewart

I prayed for a serenity of mind,
And asked for something stable and secure
To lean my weary heart upon; to bind
My broken hopes: I did not ask for more
Than some stout mast to tie my anchors to,
Or some sweet balm to soothe my wounded loves.

But you have sent this meadow, lush with dew;
The soulful evening prayers of mourning doves;
The woodsy incense of my cabin walls;
The crickets, droning chorales, a capella;
The prism'd crystal where the water falls
Above the fruited-fields, ripened and mellow.
The flame of towering hills to warm my heart
With iridescent autumn leaves afire;
These baby arms, of heaven a very part,
To still the throbbings of an old desire.

Sure as the evening sun will spend its gold
Buying the fragrant restfulness of night—
So will sunrise ever new, yet old,
Burst from the eastern hills with warming light.
And I will add one sentence to my prayer:
O thank you, God, for always being there!

Photo Opposite
Maple Leaves
FPG/Ron Thomas

The Pace That Passes Understanding

Mary E. Linton

Autumn is not a time designed for speed
After the summer's careful ripening,
Moments of quiet are the spirit's need,
And time to listen when the wood sprites sing . . .

Time to absorb the beauty and take home
Something to hold out of bright blue fall skies,
Gold leaves to hoard for days we cannot roam,
Colors that live on film when autumn dies.

Autumn is timed for little country roads
And hearts attuned to travel at their pace;
The four-lane speedways are for those who goad
All operations into one long race.

How much is lost—Life's richest, highest power—
Tearing through autumn at sixty miles an hour.

AT HARVEST

Essie L. Mariner

Earth is giving up her store of riches, a fulfillment,
    In harvests, yielding up a wealth to him that planted,
To all that worked, and all that failed to work,
    The day of reckoning has come,
        on which they counted.

There need be no repinings, or regrets, at harvest,
    What seeds were sown, what work was done, is done,
There was given time and strength, used or wasted
    God sent the rain to all, and the good sun.

The earth has taught her lesson of fulfillment,
    Living a life in one short year, this one,
Bringing her abundance to the harvest
    Of he who left no little task undone.

Prayer in Autumn

Rose Koralewsky

Thou who hast made the earth the home of God
To this Thy child, earth-lover through the years,
Forgive, if when the Golden Street appears,
Its lustre pales beside the goldenrod.

If gates of pearl and walls of porphyry-stone
And all the glories of that Heavenly Land
Evoke no wonder, spare Thy wrathful hand—
Remember autumn woods these eyes have known.

BITS & PIECES

It is the duty of all nations to acknowledge the providence of Almighty God, to obey His will, to be grateful for His benefits, and humbly to implore His protection.

George Washington

If one should give me a dish of sand and tell me there were particles of iron in it, I might look for them with my eyes, and search for them with my clumsy fingers, and be unable to detect them; but let me take a magnet and sweep through it, and how would it draw to itself the almost invisible particles by the mere power of attraction. The unthankful heart, like my finger in the sand, discovers no mercies; but let the thankful heart sweep through the day, and as the magnet finds iron, so it will find, in every hour, some heavenly blessing, only the iron in God's sand is gold.

Henry Ward Beecher

18

One can never pay in gratitude; one can only pay "in kind" somewhere else in life.

Anne Morrow Lindbergh

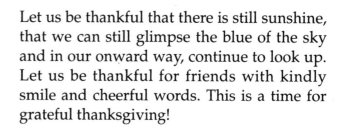

Let us be thankful that there is still sunshine, that we can still glimpse the blue of the sky and in our onward way, continue to look up. Let us be thankful for friends with kindly smile and cheerful words. This is a time for grateful thanksgiving!

Author Unknown

Make a joyful noise unto the Lord,
    all ye lands.
Serve the Lord with gladness: come before
    his presence with singing.
Know ye that the Lord he is God; it is he that
    hath made us, and not we ourselves; we
        are his people, and the sheep of his
            pasture.
Enter into his gates with thanksgiving, and
    into his courts with praise: be thankful
        unto him, and bless his name.
For the Lord is good; his mercy is
    everlasting; and his truth endureth
        to all generations.

Psalm 100

God's goodness hath been great to thee. Let never day nor night unhallowed pass but still remember what the Lord hath done.

Shakespeare

Photo Overleaf
East Orange, Vermont
Dick Dietrich Photography

Thanksgiving

Margaret Rorke

With harvest in to fill man's need,
The year from seed to bloom to seed
    Now settles down to sleep.
A sense of having done its best
Provides contentment for its rest—
    A sweet reward to reap.

Upon this day for feast and prayer,
Reviewing what we're pleased to share,
    May each of us recall
How good is gleaned from planted fields
And love provides surprising yields—
    And thank Him for it all.

Thankfulness

Elizabeth Lathrop Powers

Thankfulness is not a seasonal dress—
To wear awhile and then pack away;
It is a garment meant for daily wear,
Not just to decorate the holiday.

Its color will not fade with constant use;
The fabric will not weaken with the wear.
Each fold will keep its beauty and its strength
And all who touch it will absorb a share.

'Tis not a gown to purchase for a price,
Nor copy as to cut and fit and line;
It must be patterned by one's circumstance
And fashioned to the style of life's design.

I THANK THEE

Caroline Eyring Miner

I thank thee, Lord, for little things:

The kettle on the stove that sings;

A baby's cry; the dimpling pool

Where raindrops splatter; and the cool

Dark shadows when the day is bright;

The stars that prick the cloak of night,

And pin the sky so it won't fall;

The wondering eyes of children; all

The little seeds that lift the sod

And tell the secret that is God.

The Corn Song

John Greenleaf Whittier

Heap high the farmer's wintry hoard!
　　Heap high the golden corn!
No richer gift has Autumn poured
　　From out her lavish horn!

Let other lands, exulting, glean
　　The apple and the pine,
The orange from its glossy green,
　　The cluster from the vine;

We better love the hardy gift
   Our rugged vales bestow,
To cheer us when the storm shall drift
   Our harvest-fields with snow.

Through vales of grass and meads of flowers
   Our ploughs their furrows made,
While on the hills the sun and showers
   Of changeful April played.

We dropped the seed o'er hill and plain
   Beneath the sun of May,
And frightened from our sprouting grain
   The robber crows away.

All through the long, bright days of June
   Its leaves grew green and fair,
And waved in hot midsummer's noon
   Its soft and yellow hair.

And now, with autumn's moonlit eves,
   Its harvest time has come,
We pluck away the frosted leaves,
   And bear the treasures home.

There, when the snows about us drift,
   And winter winds are cold,
Fair hands the broken grain shall sift,
   And knead its meal of gold.

Let earth withhold her goodly root,
   Let mildew blight the rye,
Give to the worm the orchard's fruit,
   The wheat-field to the fly:

But let the good old crop adorn
   The hills our fathers trod;
Still let us, for his golden corn,
   Send up our thanks to God!

"Feeding the Chickens" by G.H. Durrie. Entered according to Act of Congress in the year 1863, by Currier & Ives, in the Clerk's Office of the District Court of the United States, for the Southern District of New York.

Over the River and through the Wood

Lydia Maria Child

Over the river and through the wood,
To grandfather's house we go;
    The horse knows the way
    To carry the sleigh
Through white and drifted snow.

Over the river and through the wood—
Oh, how the wind does blow!
    It stings the toes
    And bites the nose
As over the ground we go.

Over the river and through the wood,
To have a first-rate play.
    Hear the bells ring,
    "Ting-a-ling-ling!"
Hurrah for Thanksgiving Day!

Over the river and through the wood,
Trot fast my dapple-gray!
    Spring over the ground
    Like a hunting-hound,
For this is Thanksgiving Day!

Over the river and through the wood,
And straight through the barnyard gate.
    We seem to go
    Extremely slow—
It is so hard to wait.

Over the river and through the wood—
Now grandmother's cap I spy!
    Hurrah for the sun!
    Is the pudding done?
Hurrah for the pumpkin pie!

Pamela Kennedy

Susan dropped the three heavy grocery bags on the kitchen table. They contained the ingredients for the annual Thanksgiving dinner. As she began to unload them, her three teenagers clamored for her attention.

"Can you believe it, Mom? I mean it would have been bad enough if she had made a pass at him, but she STOLE him." Susan's daughter Amy said. "And now he is going to take her to the Thanksgiving game and dance. I could die, I could just die!" she continued as she slumped into a chair, as if to dramatize this last statement.

"You jerk!" shouted thirteen-year-old Sean as he stumbled through the doorway bearing an ice-glazed turkey. The frozen bird took flight and skidded across the kitchen floor, coming to rest in a slow spin under the table. "Mom, Brian tripped me! I was doing absolutely nothing and he tripped me!"

Before Susan could reply, the accused entered the room, grinning. His letterman's sweater hung casually over one arm as he balanced a sack of groceries in the other. "The little squirt deserved it. He said he was carrying my relative. He has got to learn to respect his elders!" Seventeen-year-old Brian stooped to give his mother a peck on the cheek, grabbed two acorn squash from the

bag, and began to juggle them.

"Squash!?" Sean shrieked. "Mom, you aren't going to make us eat squash again this year, are you?" The thirteen-year-old did a remarkable imitation of death by gagging and Susan retrieved the offending vegetables.

"Listen, all of you!" Three faces turned toward their mother in vague boredom. "It's Thanksgiving. Let's be thankful, let's show some appreciation and some gratitude."

Amy moaned. "I just told you that my life is over."

"Trash the squash and I'll show some real gratitude!"

"Mom, get real. Thanksgiving is just a boring holiday. No presents, no excitement, and we have to get all dressed up and spend hours at the table! The only good part is the football on TV."

Looking back on it, Susan was never sure which comment had done it, but singly or together, they had crystallized her determination. The idea had flashed into her mind like one of those lightbulbs in a comic strip. Suddenly, she had known exactly what she would do to give her thankless brood a different view of the holiday. Putting away the rest of her groceries, she smiled to herself.

On Thanksgiving morning she woke the children early, fed them a hearty breakfast, and piled them into the van. She refused to answer their questions and just chatted amicably when they badgered her for explanations.

They drove through the early morning traffic, past closed stores and shops, turning finally into a street that was more narrow and more dismal than the others. She stopped the van in front of a dark doorway with a peeling sign that said "THE MISSION."

"Yuk," Amy announced with a shudder.

"Mom, are you bringing a derelict home for dinner?" Brian asked.

"No," Susan replied, turning a bright smile on her handsome, healthy, middle-class children. "We are going to have a real Thanksgiving here."

They looked at her as if she had lost her mind.

"Mom, it's filthy in there! Who knows what we could catch!"

"Yes, I know," replied Susan, looking her stylish daughter straight in the eye. "I am hoping you will catch a little perspective, my darling."

"What if they get violent?" Sean offered.

"I don't believe Thanksgiving at The Mission has a reputation for violence, Sean. Let's go kids."

Like doomed prisoners, they followed her into the dining room where they met Mr. Parsons, director of The Mission. Alerted by Susan, Mr. Parsons had job assignments all ready for his "Thanksgiving Angels," as he called the gloomy trio. Ignoring their downcast faces, he put them to work setting tables, sweeping floors, and stringing orange and brown crepe paper streamers over the doorways.

By two o'clock, the dining room was ready and the guests began to arrive. Hollow-eyed teens and bag ladies, young mothers with toddlers and elderly men in layers of sweaters passed through the cafeteria line to receive steamy slices of turkey, fluffy potatoes with rich gravy, yams, squash, beans, peas, and cranberry sauce. They nodded their thanks, shyly smiled, and spoke a few words of appreciation to the young helpers.

Susan and Amy filled and refilled glasses with milk and juice while Brian dished up mashed potatoes and Sean set and cleared tables.

As the afternoon progressed, Susan watched the veneer of disgust drop from her children's eyes. Sean had two little helpers trailing along after him. Susan chuckled as she watched the thirteen-year-old teach them how to set the table.

Brian struck up a patter with the passing diners, charming them with his wit and humor—setting them at ease and dispelling their fears.

Susan looked for Amy, but could not find her. Had she ducked out in anger? She searched in the kitchen and pantry, but Amy wasn't there. Then she saw her, sitting at a table, blond head bent deep in conversation. Moving closer, Susan watched. A teenage girl, smaller than Amy, sat next to her. Her hair was brushed and sprayed in an exotic style, a streak of purple along one side. World-weary eyes glistened under iridescent lids and scarlet tipped fingers accompanied her conversation. Then Susan spied the baby, a tiny, frowning bundle in her daughter's arms. Susan left the two girls to their conversation and returned to filling empty glasses.

When the last guest was out the door and the dining room cleaned and swept, the four Thanksgiving visitors headed for home. A heavy silence filled the van as each was lost in thought.

At home, Brian handed his mother a note. "From an old man," he explained. Susan unfolded the paper and read the three-word message: "Thanks for giving."

They were only three words, but they captured the difference in this Thanksgiving. In their abundance, the little family had much to be thankful for—so much that they somehow missed the other part of what the holiday was all about. She smiled and tucked the note into her pocket, satisfied with the knowledge that her children had finally had an opportunity to discover that there could be thanks in giving, too.

Pamela Kennedy is a freelance writer of short stories, articles, essays, and children's books. Married to a naval officer and mother of three children, she has made her home on both U.S. coasts and currently resides in Hawaii. She draws her material from her own experiences and memories, adding bits of imagination to create a story or mood.

We Thank Thee

Mary E. Linton

For guidance when the night is long,
For faith that keeps hope burning strong,
And this, our heritage of song,
   We thank Thee, Lord.

For dreams that lift our hearts on wings,
For peace that understanding brings,
And for something in the soul that sings,
   We thank Thee, Lord.

Photo Opposite
Hearty Feast
Paul Polis Photography

FROM MY
G·A·R·D·E·N
JOURNAL

Deana Deck

Herb Gardens

An early evening stroll through a fragrant herb garden in mid-summer is one of the most pleasant of gardening experiences. The fragrances blend until no individual plant can be identified, and they hang heavily upon the air, inspiring images of savory dishes to be served at elaborate banquets of the imagination.

Herbs were listed in garden journals by the

first American settlers, and, for a long time after, they were widely grown and used throughout the developing country. But with the appearance of the first processed convenience foods, cooking with herbs began to fall out of favor.

In the average household in the recent past, a touch of sage or thyme in the turkey dressing at Thanksgiving or an extra clove of garlic in the spaghetti sauce has been the extent of herb use. Occasionally an adventurous hostess might pluck a sprig of fresh mint from the wild patch beside the back door and serve it tucked in a glass of iced tea, but most herbs have been all but forgotten in this country—until recent times.

Now herbs are back. One of the results of the recent emphasis on low-calorie, low-sodium cuisine has been a reawakening of interest in the use of fresh herbs. Racks of herb seed are available at nearly all garden centers, and tiny pots of herbs can even be purchased in the fresh produce department of many supermarkets, ready to use as windowsill plants or in the garden.

The flavor and interest that herbs can add to cooking is well-known, but an almost equal benefit is the fragrance and color they add to the garden. In the herb gardens of many European estates, low-growing varieties are planted among the stones in ancient paths so that as they are stepped on they will impart a rich fragrance to the air along the stroller's way. Winter savory is especially popular for this use.

Most herbs have the hardy constitutions associated with weeds and thus are not difficult for the average gardener to grow. In fact, most are native to the rocky, volcanic coasts of the Mediterranean and are tolerant of drought and poor soil. Most of the more aromatic varieties, in fact, actually do better in fair to poor soil, as slow development results in a heavier concentration of aroma in the leaf, flower, or stem. Because of this, most herbs require little or no fertilizing,

and once your garden is established you can expect it to last years with only moderate attention.

Like all plants, herbs fall into one of three categories: annuals, biennials, or perennials. Beginners should start by planting a few easy annual varieties from seed—dill, mint, or basil, for instance. Purchase small starter plants of the easier perennials, like sage, thyme, chives, or oregano. For biennials, try parsley or caraway.

Although the concept of a windowsill full of herbs is a very popular one, in truth, they are not as easy to grow indoors as they are in a sunny garden. Without supplemental lighting or a greenhouse window, these light loving plants will quickly decline.

In addition, remember that all perennials will go dormant, no matter what you do. And plants begun in the garden should not be transplanted indoors to pots; if you plan to grow herbs in pots, its better to start them in pots, since they do not take too kindly to transplanting.

Herbs are nearly pest-free: their greatest enemy outdoors is a dog in the garden. Mint may be affected by white fly, and caterpillars may get on parsley, but they can be picked off without causing damage. Nothing bothers thyme, savory, or oregano. Some herbs may actually repel insects; this fact has led to their use as companion plants to protect the vegetable garden.

Whether you decide upon a small indoor herb garden, or a more extensive outdoor patch, the rewards of herb gardening are many and long-lasting. Their color and fragrance will be a constant delight, and once you have realized the spark and personality that favorite herbs add to your menus, you will likely become an enthusiastic and devoted herb gardener.

Deana Deck lives in Nashville, Tennessee, where her garden column is a regular feature in the Tennessean.

CRAFTWORKS

HERB WREATHS

Barbara Milo Orhbach

Wreaths make the kind of gift that everyone seems to love. The ones you make yourself are even more appreciated, and since all the botanicals used in a wreath are dried, you can make several at a time to have on hand when an occasion arises.

Materials:

A **straw form** (the finished wreath will be 2 to 4 inches larger than the form, so choose the size accordingly).

Florist's pins, to attach the herbs to the form.

Sprigs of four kinds of dried herbs, 5 inches long. Use opal basil, Silver King artemisia, parsley, and sage or another combination with nice color contrast, such as lamb's ears, rosemary, Silver Lake artemisia, and tansy.

A **wire loop**, for hanging the wreath.

Making the Wreath:

1. Starting with the Silver King artemisia (or the lightest colored herb), arrange several sprigs, stems outward, to create a curved row on the form. Attach each sprig to the form with florist's pins.

2. Create a second and third row with the rest of the artemisia so that the three rows are equidistant from each other. Pin in place as before. Be sure to keep all sprigs curving in the same direction and to overlap the sprigs to hide the pins.

3. Alongside each row of the artemisia and using the same technique, make three rows each of the opal basil and the parsley or whatever herbs give the highest contrast to the first. You should now have twelve rows in all on the form.

4. Attach the wire loop to the back of the wreath for hanging.

Photo: Three steps in making and herb wreath. *Left:* The straw form. *Right:* Sprigs of artemisia and opal basil arranged in three curved rows with floral pins. *Below:* Layers of parsley and sage are added to finish.

Providence

Margaret E. Sangster

What time the latest flower hath bloomed,
　The latest bird hath southward flown;
When silence weaves o'er garnered sheaves
　Sweet idyls in our northern zone;
When scattered children rest beside
　The hearth, and hold their mother's hand,
Then rolls Thanksgiving's ample tide
　Of fervent praise across the land.

And though the autumn stillness broods
　Where spring was glad with song and stir,
Though summer's grace leave little trace
　On fields that smiled with sight of her,
Still glows the sunset's altar fire
　With crimson flame and heart of gold,
And faith uplifts, with strong desire
　And deep content, the hymns of old.

We bless our God for wondrous wealth,
　Through all the bright benignant year;
For shower and rain, for ripened grain;
　For gift and guerdon, far and near
We bless the ceaseless Providence
　That watched us through the peaceful days,
That led us home, or brought us thence,
　And kept us in our various ways.

And if the hand so much that gave
　Hath something taken from our store.
If caught from sight, to heaven's pure light,
Some precious ones are here no more,
　We still adore the Friend above,
Who, while earth's road grows steep and dim,
　Yet comforts us, in tender love,
And holds our darlings close to Him.

Thanks, then, O God! From sea to sea
　Let every wind the anthem bear!
And hearts be rife through toil and strife,
　With joyful praise and grateful prayer.
Our fathers' God, their children sing
　The grace they sought through storm and sun;
Our harvest tribute here we bring,
　And end it with, "Thy will be done."

A Thanksgiving Prayer

Judy Schwab

Give me this day
  With family and friends;
Give me a home
  Where love never ends;
Give me a smile
  For loved ones to share;
Give me strong shoulders
  For burdens to bear.

Give me a moment
  To savor this day;
Give me a lifetime
  My debts to repay;
Yes, all these I ask,
  And the reason I do
Is that as I receive
  I may give back to you.

Chrysanthemums
Dirc Nienhaus/FPG

COLLECTOR'S CORNER

Souvenir Spoons

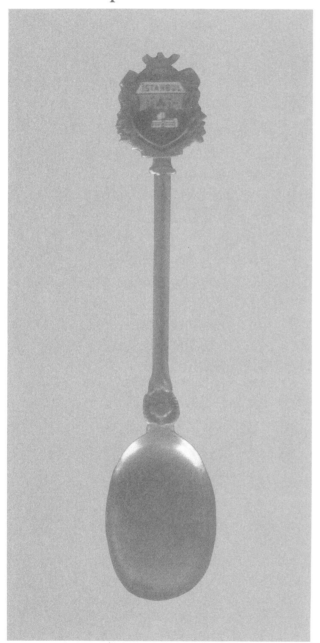

When we visit a special place or attend an important event, most of us enjoy having a memento to remind us of the occasion. That's why souvenir shops are so successful. One of the most popular souvenir items is the spoon, usually made of sterling silver or silver plate. Souvenir spoons are made for many reasons—to commemorate special occasions, to honor public personalities, as a memento of a location, or as a means of advertising—and since the late nineteenth century, they have been a consistently popular collectible.

Perhaps the reason that spoons are so sought-after is because of their history—both as a common utensil and a symbol of wealth. Their use goes far back into human history. The word "spoon" is taken from the Anglo-Saxon word "spon" which means a chip. Originally, a spoon was merely a thin, slightly-cupped chunk of wood used to dip into foods which were too liquid to eat with the hand and too thick to drink from a bowl.

In Italy during the fifteenth century, "apostle spoons" were the fad. Made of silver, these spoons had handles formed in the likeness of an apostle, and a spoon bearing the figure of a child's patron saint was considered the ideal bap-

tismal gift by the rich Venetians and Tuscans. It is from this custom that the child of wealthy parents is said to have been "born with a silver spoon in its mouth," for only the wealthy could afford to commission a silver apostle's spoon as a christening gift for their child.

Spoon collecting first became popular as a hobby in the 1890s. During that time the first patent was issued for a Niagara Falls commemorative spoon. This began a long line of spoons depicting favorite travel destinations. Spoons portraying famous people were another early form of the collectible. In 1889, a spoon with the likeness of George Washington was issued, followed later that year by one featuring his wife, Martha: to this day, spoons depicting our national heroes and celebrities remain popular. Many of these early spoons are valuable not only for their historical and sentimental value, but for their fine examples of the craftsmanship of the nineteenth-century silversmith.

Spoon collecting has remained popular, experiencing highs and lows just like any other hobby, but always maintaining a group of devoted collectors. Today, a resurgence is occurring, and people with a variety of interests and backgrounds are joining the ranks of American spoon collectors.

Some of today's collectors have only spoons that highlight their own experiences. The worth of this kind of collection is immeasurable, as

 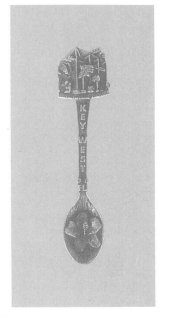

Spoons from the collection of Frances Parker, Hendersonville, Tennessee

each spoon represents an event, person, or place that has significance for the collector.

Other collectors, however, enjoy looking for unusual spoons at flea markets, estate sales, antique stores, and garage sales. For this type of collector, the highly unusual or rare spoon is an item to be prized.

When assessing souvenir spoons, collectors watch for several things: material, condition, subject, dates, and markings. Unless a damaged spoon is very rare or is needed to complete a collection, it should be avoided. Still, as with most collectibles, personal interest and need are the deciding factors in purchasing souvenir spoons.

Frames and trays for displaying a spoon collection are readily available. This, along with the relatively low cost of the spoons themselves, makes this a particularly appealing collectible. Spoon collecting can be a satisfying pastime—especially as we reflect and wonder about the events, people, and places that inspired the creation of each individual spoon and how they shaped our nation's history, or our own personal history.

Carol Shaw Johnston, a public school teacher, writes articles and short stories. She lives with her family in Brentwood, Tennessee.

43

Not Only for Our Food

Barbara McCutchen

Not only for our food today,
But for the blessings along the way—
For loved ones home from o'er the miles,
For children's hugs and babies' smiles,
For Grandma's kiss and Grandpa's pat,
For bouncing pup and sleeping cat,
For rocking chairs and hot cocoa
Near the fireside's cheery glow;

For autumn leaves beneath our feet,
For loving friends we rush to greet,
For water, sparkling, from the well
And amber mums with spicy smell.
For cars and trucks and ships and planes,
For umbrellas when it rains,
For twinkling stars, the moon that glows,
The sun that beams and wind that blows;

For woolly coats and mittens warm,
And home—our shelter in a storm;
For health and wealth and joy and love,
For God's good favor from above,
For blessings great and blessings small
We thank you, Lord, for one and all.

GOING HOME

Angela Gall

A hundred miles of singing roads
Where hill-capped farmlands fall and rise
With gaping bins of yellow grain,
Pumpkin gold and harvest skies,
Then the hill-home the heart knows so well,
The warmth where open arms await,
The sweets and spice all nostril-nice,
The turkey-cranberry laden plate—
This feast with loved ones a world away,
All mine by journey of heart today

HOMING

Betty W. Stoffel

If God can teach such tiny birds
Their homeward flight in spring,

It is no wonder human souls
Are softly set a-wing,

And held to course through heaven's space
By some compelling thing;

For there must be some inborn sight
That sets the soul in homeward flight.

Cranberry Season

The golden roasted turkey, stuffed with a savory dressing and teamed with a tangy cranberry sauce, will be the star of many Thanksgiving tables. But the sparkling cranberry is capable of so much more—for dessert, try this wonderful autumn fruit in pies. Our Cranberry Lattice Pie is flavored with maple syrup and laced with wheat germ and flaked coconut, and our second pie teams cranberries with crisp fall apples for a unique and delectable flavor combination. Either one will add a special touch to your Thanksgiving meal, and both are guaranteed to make you and your family devoted fans of the cranberry.

Cranberry Lattice Pie

  | pastry for 2-crust pie
12 | ounces fresh cranberries
1 1/2 | tablespoons cornstarch
1/2 | cup wheat germ
1 | cup flaked coconut
1 | cup maple syrup

Preheat oven to 450°. Line a 9-inch pie plate with half the pastry. In a large bowl, combine the remaining ingredients, blending well. Turn into a pastry-lined pie plate. Roll remaining pastry into a 10-inch circle. Cut into 3/4-inch strips. Place on top of pie in lattice fashion. Turn and flute edges.

Bake for 10 minutes at 450°. Reduce oven temperature to 350°; bake an additional 25-30 minutes, or until crust is golden. Serves eight.

Apple Cranberry Pie

1 | 10-inch unbaked pie shell

Filling
1 | egg
1 | cup dairy sour cream
1 | cup sugar
3 | tablespoons cornstarch
2 | teaspoons vanilla
1/2 | teaspoon salt
2 1/2 | pounds cooking apples
1 | cup cranberries, washed and drained

Topping
1/2 | cup flour
1/3 | cup sugar
1/3 | cup brown sugar
2 | teaspoons cinnamon
1/4 | teaspoon salt
1/2 | cup butter or margarine
1 | cup chopped walnuts

Preheat oven to 425°. Beat egg slightly in a large bowl. Add sour cream, sugar, cornstarch, vanilla, and salt. Stir until combined. Pare and thinly slice apples into mixture. Stir in cranberries.

To prepare topping, combine flour, sugars, cinnamon, and salt. Cut butter into dry ingredients. Stir in walnuts. Spoon apple mixture into prepared pastry crust. Sprinkle topping evenly over filling. Place pie on bottom rack of oven; bake 10 minutes. Lower heat to 350°; bake 50 minutes longer. Cool. Serves eight to ten.

Bonnie Aeschliman is a teacher of occupational home economics and a freelance food consultant. She lives in Wichita, Kansas, with her husband and their two children.

Photo courtesy of Ocean Spray

John Slobodnik

A SLICE OF LIFE

Edgar A. Guest

Forefathers' Day

Look back three hundred years and more:
A group upon a rock-bound shore,
Borne by the Mayflower o'er the sea,
Pledged hearts and lives to liberty.

They were the few we hail with pride
Singing: "Land where our fathers died,"
Daring to die that this might be
Forever: "Land of the noble free."

At Plymouth Rock they could not know
How far their shadows then would go,
That freedom (as today we sing)
From every mountainside should ring.

"Our Fathers' God to Thee" I pray
That we, devoted as were they,
Who sing: "Long may our land be bright"
Shall cherish: "Freedom's holy light."

Edgar A. Guest began his career in 1895 at the age of fourteen when his work first appeared in the Detroit Free Press. *His column was syndicated in over 300 newspapers, and he became known as "The Poet of the People."*

Time to Give Thanks

Give thanks to our God for all He
sends with love,
there are your children, your home,
loved ones and friends—there's His comfort
He gives in times of need and sorrow,
the beauty we see each and every day.
Give thanks for the returning of morning's
light, the sun that shines brightly for us
and the stars glittering at night.
For all these things we should lift
our eyes, open our hearts to our
Lord giving thanks. Amen!

Carolynn Mitchell
Saucier, Mississippi

Thanksgiving Musings

Turkey, whole or sliced;
Tea, iced or spiced;
Broccoli, steamed or riced;
Make Thanksgiving nice.

Family, far or near;
Friends, loved and dear;
Relationships, known and clear;
People, loved, who have no peers.

Time, relaxing, having fun;
Work, embarked upon and done;
Battles, fought and won;
Wondrous day, from rising to setting sun.

Wanda Bracken
Lawton, Oklahoma

Reflections

Autumn Rainbows

We thank you, God, Our Father,
For the beauty in the world.
Especially each autumn,
When your colors are unfurled.

The crispness of the weather
Brings the colors from within.
As leaves portray Your splendor
How we love to take it in!

Dear God, we, too, have beauty
Sometimes shielded, out of view.
How we long to show our colors
And reflect the joy of You.

But sometimes cares and worries
Make our vision dulled and gray
And the colors of Your presence
Don't shine forth in grand display.

So teach us, Lord, to listen,
To honor, and obey.
Help us to share You freely
As we travel on life's way.

Give our lives real inner beauty.
Thank You for forgiving sin.
Let us share the joy of Jesus
And not keep the beauty in.

Jill Perkins
Cassopolis, Michigan

Thanksgiving Memories

D.A. Hoover

Across corn fields and woods I walked
  One crisp Thanksgiving Day
To Grandma's house for dinner
  With lots of time to play.

The cold wind rattled empty husks
  A few clouds floated high,
I heard the honk and saw the V
  Of wild geese flying by.

A cottontail bobbed down a row
  Quail roared up by the hedge,
Small chickadees flew out ahead
  And led me to the edge

Of Grandpa's woods, where hickory trees
   Shag-barked and tall and grey
Had dropped a crop of sweet, white nuts
   Where red fox squirrels play.

I kicked deep leaves of cinnamon
   And heard the raucous jay
Jawing behind a white-oak grove
   His music for the day.

Deep leaf mold sank beneath my tread
   A flash of tangerine
Where bittersweet and wild grape
   Grew verdantly between.

I savored hickory smoke and saw
   The house, the windmill wheel,
And thanked God for Thanksgiving Day
   And how good it made me feel.

Gratitude Remembered

June Masters Bacher

We used to gather round the fire
To join our hands in prayer;
Thanksgiving time was drawing near—
The feel was in the air.

The roof was patched, the cellar filled,
The winter wood piled high;
The cabin chinked against the cold—
Why fear the darkening sky?

Our hearts were filled with gratitude
For garners of the fall
And for the God in heaven who
Provided for us all.

Nathaniel Hawthorne

In 1692, a strange fervor gripped the Puritan citizens of Salem Village, Massachusetts. There was witchcraft among them, they believed; the devil had come into their midst and threatened to destroy their community from the inside, capturing the minds and souls of their neighbors and turning their model settlement into a chaotic battleground.

In their panic, the citizens of Salem Village looked to their leaders in Salem Town—the men who ran their churches and government—for guidance. One such leader was John Hathorne, a judge in Salem's court. Descendant from one of Massachusetts' first settlers, Judge Hathorne was a man known and respected throughout the community, and in this time of fear and uncertainty, he was entrusted with the task of pronouncing judgment upon the men and women accused of serving the devil in Massachusetts.

Hathorne sent many of the accused to Salem Jail and some to their deaths on Gallows Hill. Yet when one of those so sentenced turned to the judge as she was led away and pronounced a curse upon him and his family, it was seen as neither a threat nor a cause for guilt; rather, the curse pronounced upon Judge Hathorne was further proof to the people of Salem of the righteousness of his actions, and of the reality of the threat to the God-fearing people of the colony. Judge Hathorne was known as a brave and wise man—a heroic servant of God and country.

More than one hundred years later, on July 4, 1804, Judge John Hathorne's great grandson, Nathaniel Hawthorne, was born. The Hawthorne family still lived in Salem; but the "w" that they had added to their name was symbolic of the changes that had occurred since the elder Judge Hathorne had brought the family to prominence. For in 1804, the late judge was no hero. The tide had turned, and public opinion looked back upon the witchcraft hysteria as a black spot in local history. The curse upon Judge Hathorne, it would seem, was to be carried out after all—upon his memory.

This is not surprising. Salem in the nineteenth century bore little resemblance to the seventeenth-century city of the Puritans. An influx of settlers from different religious and cultural backgrounds had diversified the city and created a new social order. In this modern Salem, the original Puritan settlers were belittled for the narrowness of their vision and the austerity of their lifestyle. Those convicted of witchcraft had been exonerated, and the days of the witchcraft hysteria had come to symbolize the entire Puritan culture of Salem's past. Fact had been muted into legend, and the villains of the legend were the men who had led the community, men like Judge John Hathorne.

For young Nathaniel, quiet and introspective by nature and tied closely to local history by birth, the burden of the Hawthorne past was a heavy one. As long as he stayed in Salem, the shadow of his great grandfather—and all that he had come to represent in modern Salem—loomed darkly overhead.

A young man struggling with such a burden might certainly be expected to break away from his roots and strike out on his own in a new environment, some other place where he would not be defined by the history of his name. But though he would leave Salem several times in his life,

Nathaniel Hawthorne never did abandon his roots; always, he felt compelled to return to the city of his forebearers. In fact, the work of Hawthorne's adult life—the novels and his stories that made him one of our great American authors—was in large part devoted to an exploration of Salem and American colonial history.

Through his writing, Hawthorne returned to the days of Judge John Hathorne and to the Puritan world of Salem's past. So absorbed in that world was much of his work—*The Scarlet Letter* and "Young Goodman Brown" for example—that many today might mistakenly place the author in the seventeenth century. Hawthorne built his fiction out of the places, names, and events of early American colonial history and used the resulting historical drama to examine the moral dilemmas that all ages have in common. What Hawthorne displayed through his work was an understanding of the real and powerful links between past and present. His obsession with local history may have shaped his fiction, but his motives were universal.

In Hawthorne's diaries and letters, he makes mention of his struggle to come to terms with his great grandfather. As an adult, the younger Hawthorne came to respect the judge; he accepted him as neither a hero nor a villain, but as a man of his own time who acted according to his conscience in the name of public good.

And this is perhaps the most valuable lesson to be learned from Hawthorne's writing, and his life. While his plots concern the people and events of history, his intent was never simply to judge these people or events. His aim, rather, was to enlighten the present through a thorough understanding of the past. Hawthorne was one of the first American authors to closely examine the distinctly American character, and he was so successful because he understood that the character was the product of all aspects of American history, and that nineteenth-century Americans were indebted to the American settlers of the seventeenth century, just as Nathaniel Hawthorne was indebted to his own ancestors, Judge John Hathorne included. The present, Hawthorne reminds us, is never qualified to condemn the past; we all share the responsibility to learn from those who have gone before us.

Nancy J. Skarmeas

Artists rendition of the witchcraft trial of George Jacobs

The Salem Witch House

Salem, Massachusetts

When I think of Salem, Massachusetts, the first thing that leaps to mind is the witchcraft hysteria of the 1690s. This is probably true for most of us—schoolroom history lessons and popular legend have combined to lock Salem forever in the austere seventeenth-century world of the Puritans. But those of us who allow scattered bits of historical fact and legend to shape our view of this original American seaport are doing a disservice both to the city of Salem and to ourselves. History is, of course, a necessary theme of any visit to Salem, but the history to be found here extends far beyond the year 1692 and the Puritan settlers: Salem today is a living record of an American city's development from its original settlement through the twentieth century.

When you arrive in Salem, park your car and set out on foot, or take advantage of the trolley car. A walking tour is a particularly good choice, for these are three-hundred-year-old streets, narrow and winding, and only on foot are you guaranteed a comprehensive tour.

Although almost every corner of Salem holds something of interest, Chestnut Street is a good starting place for a first tour. The houses along this street were built by sea captains in the nineteenth century, when Salem was America's foremost seaport, and their size and splendor attest to Salem's early prosperity as the new nation's central harbor. Some of the homes along Chestnut Street are open to the public and many house collections of antiques and historical artifacts. One such home is the Stephen Phillips Memorial Trust House, which holds a beautiful collection of furniture and has an adjacent carriage house brimming with antique carriages and automobiles. Most homes here require an appointment to tour the inside, but even without venturing through any doors, this street is a wonderful experience. These grand old houses are unlike anything else ever built in this country, and they combine to make Chestnut Street one of the most architecturally fascinating streets in America.

Photo Overleaf
Cottonwood Trees
Canyon de Chelles National Monument
Arizona
Dick Dietrich Photography

But Chestnut Street is by no means the location of all of Salem's historic dwellings. The Pickering House on nearby Broad Street was built in 1651, and is currently the oldest house in America continually occupied by members of a single family. The home is not a museum, but it is open to the public. Inside are antiques and paintings from throughout the home's history and a collection of letters from George Washington and other prominent American men and women.

And scattered about Salem, on busy main thoroughfares and quiet, winding side streets, are houses—still serving as homes to Salem families—dating back as far as 1642. These are as old as any American homes, and they offer self-contained lessons in the development of American architecture—often evidenced in a single home added to and renovated throughout the years, with each new addition reflecting the taste of the age, and all melding into one amazingly coherent whole. And while these homes are old, they are also meticulously maintained: Salem takes its history very seriously.

Part of this history is, of course, the city's infamous battle with witchcraft. The Salem Witch Museum, the Witch Dungeon Museum, and the Witch House are all dedicated to providing an objective view of the events of the early 1690s. Visitors might be surprised to learn that most of the people involved in the witchcraft accusations and trials were actually residents of nearby Salem Village (now Danvers); but the trials themselves were held in Salem, and it is in Salem that these years are memorialized. In the Witch Dungeon, visitors can view live recreations of the trials; the Witch House is the restored home of Jonathan Corwin, one of the judges who presided at the Salem trials.

It is the Witch Museum, however, that provides the most fascinating glimpse into Salem's past. Here, visitors experience a multi-sensory presentation recreating the witchcraft hysteria from its initiation by young girls in Salem Village through the trials, executions, and ultimate end to this dark period in colonial history. Thirteen stage sets surrounding a central viewing area tell the story in amazingly life-like detail. This presentation separates fact from legend and will leave you with a much deeper understanding of Salem's infamous historical interlude.

Yet for all its history, Salem is more than just an educational experience. This is a thriving modern city, small enough not to intimidate visitors, but large enough to offer a complete range of activities. In the warmer months, visitors can stroll down Pickering Wharf, a refurbished waterfront marketplace of shops and restaurants. There is also the Peabody Museum—America's oldest—with its internationally-renowned maritime, ethnological, and natural history collections. For dining you might try the Lyceum Restaurant. Although this too is an historic site—the Lyceum Hall was once the host of such distinguished lecturers as Hawthorne, Emerson, and Thoreau, and Alexander Graham Bell's first public demonstration of the telephone took place here—it is a unique and pleasurable dining experience as well.

Salem's age and diversity make it resistant to simple characterization. This city—along with those that surround it—has been around since America's very beginning, and each age has left its mark. Yet the flavor of the place, I must admit, remains that of the seventeenth century, and it is a powerful and distinctive flavor, one that permeates the entire surrounding region.

Salem is at its best in the autumn. In this quiet time of the year, when the weather has turned colder and when the Thanksgiving holiday turns us to reflection, it is appropriate to look back upon our past and the events and people that have shaped our present. And there is no better place to do this than in Salem, where our American history awaits discovery.

Parlor, Gardner-Pingree House

63

I AM GRATEFUL

Lee Avery

I am grateful for the warmth
Of family and of friends;
For love and its calm wonder—
For all life's subtle blends.

And for the delicate surprise
Of all familiar things;
For every corner of the world
Where sudden beauty sings.

For that unwithered flower: hope;
For faith's brave candlelight
That lifts the heart and shines the way
Through the darkest night.

Country
CHRONICLE
— Lansing Christman —

Despite the tears and heartaches, despite the grief and the sorrow that come into all lives, at this Thanksgiving I consider myself fortunate. I have had the best of two worlds, and I am well along into my third.

Spring has been mine: the youthful years of awe and wonder; surprise and discovery. Like the dawn, youth is always fresh and vibrant.

Then there was my summer and my maturing and ripening in the season of longer light. This is

a quiet and sedate time, like the midday hours.

And now it is my autumn. This is the most reflective time. It is the culmination of a long span of years. It is my evening, and the transformation is profound.

I still rise before dawn to salute the light as it begins to paint the pink of dawn over the eastern horizon. I watch the stars of night fade from the skies as darkness dims. I have the daytime sun—its warmth and kindness; and I have those hours after the colors of the ebbing day give way to darkness again.

For my part, I have blended the three into an enduring symphony. There is the merging of faith and hope—blending of dreams, some lost, some gained.

Youth, maturity, and age are all essential in the composition of a lifetime. Out of these, I have composed my own personal symphony of life: the exuberant morning melodies, a perfect blend of the sedate chords of noontime's pause, and the rich refrain of evening, tender and tranquil.

The author of two published books, Lansing Christman has been contributing to Ideals *for almost twenty years. Mr. Christman has also been published in several American, foreign, and braille anthologies. He lives in rural South Carolina.*

Chrysanthemums

Mary T. McGowan

Soft white, amber, gold:
Chysanthemums grace
My tall, crystal vase.
Warm at the window,
They watch, trembling;
Indian summer's gone,
And leaves on the ground
Create a special
Patchwork quilt of
Crimson red and nutmeg brown
In the garden.

Only these scant few
Last flowers
Could I rescue
Before frost and promised snow
Would capture and steal away
Their loveliness.
Now they reign indoors,
A little longer—
These graying, blustery days—
And in glad return,
With still-fresh
Unspoiled beauty
Light up the room for me.

50 YEARS AGO

Tucking in the Farm for Winter

Back in America's country, men still cock their heads, squint at the sky, sniff the rising wind and look for "fallin' weather." The harvest moon has come and gone. Barn lofts are heavy this year with hay. Airy cribs strain their high foundations under a load of shucked yellow and white corn. Full silos breathe forth fermentation. Cellars musty through the long summer give off the sweet smell of hard-ripe apples, winter pears, pumpkins, newly dug potatoes, cider and aging home-made wine. Pantries are personal warehouses of kitchen canned beans, corn and tomatoes, fruits from the orchard and vine. Jams and jellies dance attendance upon yeast bread, biscuit, and hot cakes. Each freshening wind from the north heralds the approach of Winter's siege, when farms, large and small, become islands of humanity in a waste of snow, sleet, and ice.

Many farms today are blessed with life lines of surfaced roads, telephones, electricity, cars, rural free delivery, a weekly trip to "the store" for coffee, flour, sugar, navy beans, and tobacco, and a good gab at the "feed store," the farmers combined "Town Hall" and "Information Desk." Times have changed. Winter no longer bears the onus it did in grandfather's day.

It remains, nevertheless, a threefold problem of "planned" preparation. Homes must have fuel for heat. Livestock must be housed. Food must be stored to feed family and animals prior to the entrance of Old Man Winter, who, impervious to either defense programs or the loss of young strong hands to the service of the nation, threatens snow, ice and interminable rain, sufficient to cut off the most reliable supplies, to isolate "Ma, Pa and the kids," not forgetting the team of horses, the cows, chickens and pigs.

Under pressure of lowering thermometers and glowering skies, activity shrinks from "total" use of all outdoors to a restricted and unending circle: house to shed to barn to hen house, the telltale paths lie in the snow as day after day the same big, medium and little overshoes go about their appointed tasks. This is the season of the year when life begins and ends at home. Undisturbed by the pressure of field work, the farmer has time to recondition farm machinery, clean out the shed, inventory the toolhouse, help the Missus repaper the parlor, do over the woodwork in the house, get around to this and that "hollerin' for a fixin'."

Winter's siege is feeding time for the farmer's wife. She feeds her always hungry fami-

ly. She feeds the stoves, both cook and "set stoves." She feeds her flock of chickens. But this is a short horse soon curried after Summer's gardening, canning, and the raising of young stock. It is pure respite with the older children in school and the babies twittering over their toys on the sunny side of the kitchen. She plies her needle through quilt patches, clothes, and fresh linens. She crochets yards of cotton into bedspreads, knits up balls of wool into socks and mittens, visits through many an hour with her neighbor over the ridge, her friend down the road. She has something for the schoolchildren to eat when they pile out of the schoolbus at dusk and she sends them to their evening chores. The boys fill the kindling box, bring in a wheelbarrow load of wood. The girls set the supper table, lay out the dishes.

Today wars encircle the earth. Governments rise and teeter. Peoples work, fight, suffer at an intense, grinding pace. No matter how reversed the political and economic times, how threatening the future, Winter is a-comin', a hard, cold, despairing Winter for those who have had no summer of peace, no harvest. Here at home, our American farmers, thankful for the bounties of recent months, will lead a quiet, self-sufficient, independent existence until Spring brings fresh life to the soil, a new growing season.

The New York Times Magazine, December 15, 1940
Copyright © 1940 by The New York Times Company. Reprinted by permission

Late November

Milly Walton

November's a crone,
  withered and spent,
Mumbling on doorsteps
  in her discontent,
Grieving for days
  that will not come again,
Weeping her dismal tears
  on the pane;

She holds the last faded leaf
  to her breast
Moaning in minor tones
  full of unrest;
She drags her drab tatters
  over the land
Casting a spell
  by the touch of her hand;

She wanders the desolate
  field and hill,
Forlornly seeking
  blossom, still,
Until she finds peace
  in winter's first snow
And dreams as she sleeps
  of joy long ago.

Changing Seasons
Camerique Stock Photography

Fire's Enduring Message

Martha Byrd

This morning, in celebration of the season's first frost, I have lighted a fire in the fireplace. This has become my annual ritual for pulling the present that surrounds me into harmony with the past that has shaped me.

The house where I grew up, half a century ago, was heated by wood stoves. "Go pick up chips," my mother would say, for my wintertime chore was to gather small kindling for starting the morning fires. I have since suspected that this was busywork, designed primarily to keep me out of mischief, for my father kept a well-stocked box of heart-pine kindling beside the stove. I used to watch him splitting wood, his left hand holding a pine knot at just the proper angle against the chopping block, right hand gripping the axe close to its head. The knots split along their contorted grain with a sharp crack that zinged through the cold to strike the splintery walls of the woodshed and bounce back to meet the soft thud sounded by the axe blade when it struck the chopping block.

Crack, thud; crack, thud. He would get a rhythm going, the left hand steadily turning and advancing the uncut pine closer to the falling blade. Once I tried to hold the axe in my hand, just to see if I could, but it dropped and I had to dance out of its way to keep from being cut.

When my mother touched the wood with a lighted match, it released its stored up energy into flame. A little plume of smoke invariably trailed off the end to carry the smell of burning resin to every corner of the house. Penetrating my unheated room, the smell assured me that I would meet warmth when I left the cozy

security of my bed.

These fires in my childhood formed the nucleus for the whole family's activities, for only the great room was kept warm throughout the day. Whatever our needs, we assembled there, united by the fire's crackling companionship. Coming in from outdoors, we stood around the stove and talked, saturating our senses with the heat, the aroma of sassafras tea—or possibly a pot of beans—that simmered on top of the stove, with the sound of the steam singing its way out of the copper kettle.

Warmed and satisfied, we would settle back down to our endeavors. My mother's chair sat between the stove and a sunny window, which lighted her constant handiwork. I learned how to sew by hanging over her shoulder. Occasionally, when there was a quilt in the making, her friends might join her around the frame while I made my playhouse underneath. If I could stay quiet long enough, they would forget that I was there.

On winter evenings, my parents read the newspaper or listened to the radio. I never realized, of course, that we were poor, understanding only that something they called a depression caused them much worry. When the president spoke, we drew our chairs close to listen. I imagined him as another member of the family—how else could he have known that we sat by the fire seeking reassurance from its warmth and from the words that he spoke. Had he come to the door, I would have welcomed him without surprise.

This morning, my firewood is still green. The logs hiss with the heat. In the quiet, I recall favorite words from Kipling's *Recessional*: "Be with us yet, lest we forget." I realize that these are the words that have compelled me through the years, the words that drive my career as a historian. Perhaps I first read them on one of those winter evenings by the great room stove; today they surface as the message from my ritual fire. We are, indeed, a part of all we have met.

Photo Overleaf
Newark, Vermont
Fred M. Dole Productions

Thanksgiving for No

Carol Bessent Hayman

This year I thank you, Lord,
   for things that seemed not given.
It is so easy to give thanks for food,
For shelter, for loved ones near:
These I can touch and see.
I give you thanks instead
   for all the No's that you have said.

I am a willful one,
   inclined to feel I know the way ahead.
Thank you for keeping
   these poor stumbling feet
From all the worldly pleasures
   they could find.

Thank you for guiding me along a path,
Much harder, Lord,
   than I thought I could climb,
And thank you most of all for saying No!
   when I would faint and fall,
To let another shoulder my heart's load.
You gave me strength,
   you taught me patience, love;
And so on this Thanksgiving Day,
Thank you, Lord,
   for every time this wonderful year
When you said No.

Readers' Forum

Did you know that it is very doubtful there is anyone who is more thrilled to receive your lovely magazine—than the woman who is writing you? Every copy is like a breath of fresh air, and the photos are so beautiful they are worthy of being framed. Some dear friends of mine have given me as subscription for several years—one of the most thoughtful gifts I have ever received!

Ruth M. Comstock
La Jolla, California

I received my first copy of Ideals *and was so impressed with each page, which prompted me to read from cover to cover. I immediately wrote a check for my full year . . . and also sent a check for my best friend who lives in a city, not beautiful country as I do and will really appreciate the beauty of your* Ideals.

Lee Lashbrook
Arnold, California

I used to think that Ideals *was just an "old lady's" magazine, so I wasn't too thrilled when I received a gift subscription from my father. I'm only forty—not an "old lady" yet! But was I wrong! The beautiful pictures and stories bring back my childhood days. I know why my mother enjoyed the magazine, and I know I will pass the tradition of* Ideals *to my children, too.*

Carolyn Phillips
Des Moines, Iowa

My friend has loaned me her treasures—her Ideals*—for years. I've noticed in recent months they have travel, many essays, crafts, hobbies, etc. . . Don't take up the pages with all this other stuff. Nowhere can you get a magazine like* Ideals*—the breathtaking pictures and sonnets—keep* Ideals *unique!*

Hilda J. Lairamore

Editor's Note: Readers are invited to submit unpublished, original poetry, short anecdotes, and humorous reflections on life for possible publication in *Ideals* issues. Please send copies only; manuscripts will not be returned. Writers receive $10 for each published submission. Send material to "Readers' Reflections," Ideals Publishing Corporation, P.O. Box 140300, Nashville, Tennessee 37214-0300.

Want to share your crafts?
Readers are invited to submit original craft ideas for possible development and publication in future *Ideals* issues. Please send query letter (with photograph if possible) to Editorial Features Department, Ideals Publishing Corporation, P.O. Box 140300, Nashville, Tennessee 37214-0300. Please do not send craft samples; they cannot be returned.

ideals
Celebrating Life's Most Treasured Moments